cool science

Sports Technology

Ron Fridell

LERNER BOOKS • LONDON • NEW YORK • MINNEAPOLIS

First published in the United Kingdom in 2009 by
Lerner Books,
Dalton House,
60 Windsor Avenue,
London SW19 2RR

Website address: www.lernerbooks.co.uk

This edition was updated and edited for UK publication by Discovery Books Ltd.,
Unit 3, 37 Watling Street, Leintwardine, Shropshire SY7 0LW

British Library Cataloguing in Publication Data

Fridell, Ron
Sports technology. - (Cool science)
1. Sports sciences - Juvenile literature 2. Sports -
Technological innovations - Juvenile literature 3. Sporting
goods - Juvenile literature
I. Title
688.7'6

ISBN-13: 978 0 7613 4299 1

Printed in Singapore

Table of Contents

Introduction

Athletes keep getting faster and stronger. The winner of the first Olympic marathon ran the 40-kilometre (25-mile) course in just under three hours. That was in 1896. Modern athletes can run a marathon nearly 60 minutes faster – and modern marathons are nearly two kilometres longer.

This marathon took place in Brooklyn, New York, USA, in 1909.

The same goes for other competitive sports. Cyclists, skiers, football players, swimmers and pole vaulters keep setting new records, thanks to improved physical training, health care and eating habits.

These improvements are only part of the story, however. Let's not forget sports technology – the tools, machines and materials that make good athletes even better. Space-age metals boost pole vaulters to new heights. Bioengineered bodysuits inspired by sharks help competitive swimmers set speed records. High-tech artificial legs give athletes without flesh-and-bone limbs the chance to become champion professional sprinters.

These athletes are competing in the New York Marathon. The man on the right went on to win with a time of 2:09:04.

Sports technology also helps people who are not professional athletes. It helps keep them safe and comfortable as they ride and run. Sports technology puts more fun into activities such as bike riding and golf and more thrills into big-wave surfing, hang gliding and other daring pursuits. Hang on tight as we take a fast-moving journey through the world of sports technology.

Chapter 1

Get Better and Better

Some sports technology helps make competitive athletes better. New inventions and materials such as space-age metals help improve performance. These are some of the same metals used in spacecraft. That means that astronauts and Olympic pole vaulters share something in common. Both defy gravity with the help of space-age metals.

Energy Released

Vaulters in the 1896 Olympics used bamboo poles to propel themselves upwards towards a crossbar. A half century later, poles made of thin strands of glass called fibreglass sent vaulters soaring to new heights. Then, in the 1960s, aluminium poles helped lift them still higher.

Modern poles are made of carbon fibre, thread-like strands of carbon atoms sealed in heated plastic. Spacecraft and vaulting poles both contain carbon fibre because it is so lightweight and superstrong.

Carbon fibre poles also bend more easily and that bending generates more stored energy. As the running vaulter plants the pole and leaps, the pole bends in a backward arc. Energy is stored in the pole as it bends. As the pole springs forwards, that energy is released. It propels the vaulter up, up, up and over the crossbar.

The more energy the pole can store and release, the higher the vaulter can leap. The 1896 Olympic record of 3.2 metres was achieved with a bamboo pole. The top modern vaulters easily clear 6 m with their high-energy, space-age poles.

Modern pole vaulters use poles made of carbon fibre, which bends easily and stores energy to help propel the vaulter to new heights.

Technology and Technique

Early pole vaulters came down hard on their feet in a landing pit of sawdust or sand. When new, improved poles sent them higher, they needed softer places to land. So pits were filled with foam-filled bags and foam mats.

Pole vaulting technique also had to change. As vaulters soared higher and fell further, they became like acrobats. No longer did they travel straight up and down, feet first. Instead, modern pole vaulters twist and turn in mid-air. As a result, these acrobatic athletes clear the crossbar head first facing the sky and then land on their backs or shoulders.

Vaulters use poles to hurl their bodies skywards. Tennis players and golfers use rackets and clubs to send round objects flying through the air.

The first tennis rackets had frames and handles made of wood. Then came steel and aluminium. Most modern rackets are composites – two or more materials bound together. Many tennis pros use rackets that contain graphite and Kevlar. Graphite, a soft form of carbon, is the same material used to make the 'lead' in pencils. Kevlar is five times stronger than steel.

Together, these soft and tough materials make the racket both lighter and stronger. That added power helps tennis players hit the ball harder. Modern professional players can serve a tennis ball at speeds well over 160 kph (100 mph). Composite rackets also give players more control.

Bjorn Borg
Tennis legend Bjorn Borg (right) won 11 Grand Slam titles in the 1970s and 1980s. He used a wooden racket. In 1991 he made a comeback with a wooden racket, but he was soundly beaten by a little-known player using a graphite racket.

Professional golfers prefer clubs made of the space-age metal titanium. Like carbon fibre and Kevlar, titanium is lightweight and high in strength. That means added power and control for the golfer.

I Can Do This Better

New sports technologies don't just pop up overnight. An inventor with a smart idea must have the ambition and skill to put in the hard work to make it real.

Howard Head, an aircraft engineer, was one of those ambitious inventors. Head got his bright idea during a skiing holiday. He realized that the sport of skiing would be more fun if the wooden skis he was using were easier to control. That way, the skier could make smoother, sharper turns.

I can build a better ski, he decided, and that's just what Howard Head did. He coated a wood core with aluminium and plastic and added steel edges.

Then he had a prototype, a model that needed testing. Head was not a good skier, so he handed the skis over to a professional ski instructor. Then he

Howard Head developed a better ski. Later, he went on to develop a better tennis racket.

watched as the instructor zigzagged expertly down the mountainside and glided smoothly to a stop.

'They're great, Mr. Head, just great,' the instructor told him.

And so they were. That was more than 60 years ago. Howard Head's company still makes skis, but they are far better than that first prototype. Modern skis are stronger, lighter, and even easier to move. They have better designs and are built of titanium, carbon fibre and other materials originally developed by the aerospace industry.

Goal: A Superfast Bicycle

The first bicycles were made about 200 years ago. Back then, bikes were just a way of getting around. No one saw cycling as an athletic event.

By the 1940s, bike racing was an international sport. What was once a simple way of getting around had become a complex, high-tech competition. The ultimate goal was speed. That meant building a more lightweight bike based on aerodynamics. Aerodynamics is the study of how air flows around a moving body. The flow of air resists, or slows, a bicycle's forward progress. The more air resistance the harder the rider must work to move forwards. If you cut down the bike's resistance to air, then the rider can move at a higher speed using less energy.

The RMIT Superbike was built to cut through the air. It was designed for the 1996 Australian Olympics team. The head of the design team was an aerospace engineer. This ambitious team set out to create a strong, light, aerodynamically superior bicycle with the precision and quality of a fighter jet.

This member of the 1996 Australian Olympics team is racing an RMIT Superbike.

How They Created It

To test aerodynamics, the team used a wind tunnel. The bike was bolted to a platform, with a dummy in place of a real rider. As a motor beneath the tunnel's floor drove the wheels, the dummy rider's Styrofoam legs and feet rose and fell with the pedals. A machine blew air through the tunnel at different speeds while scientific instruments measured the bike's resistance to wind.

Engineers used carbon fibre, Kevlar and other space-age materials to make the bike's frame lighter. They kept changing the bike's design to reduce the aerodynamic resistance. Finally, the team was satisfied.

The Superbike design team reached its goal. Competitive athletes loved it. In a four-year span, Superbike riders won 23 world championships and set three world records.

Swimmers and Sharks

Why would scientists who wanted to help people swim faster study sharks? Their thinking went this way: Sharks have evolved over millions of years to become some of the fastest swimmers on the planet. That's quite a feat. So let's work out how sharks do it. What lessons can we learn about moving faster through the water from these superswimmers?

Researchers decided that reducing water resistance was the key. The same sort of thing that happens to bicycle riders in the air happens to swimmers in the water. The fastest swimmers do the best job of reducing the water's resistance to their bodies' movement through the water.

Researchers discovered how sharks manage to do this. As they swim, sharks stretch their skin and change its texture so that water flows more freely over and around it. A swimsuit company, Speedo, used these discoveries to design full bodysuits. These swimsuits act like the skin of a shark.

A Second Skin

Full bodysuits are constructed of separate panels. Each panel covers a different group of muscles that work together as the swimmer moves along. The panels are like a second skin. Each one expands and contracts independently, on its own. This makes the swimmer's body more sleek and compact, which produces less resistance to the water.

Researchers also discovered that a shark's skin has a unique texture. The full bodysuit's fabric, called Fastskin, imitates this texture. Like a shark's skin, Fastskin is made of little pointed ridges facing in different directions. The ridges pull water in and reduce resistance.

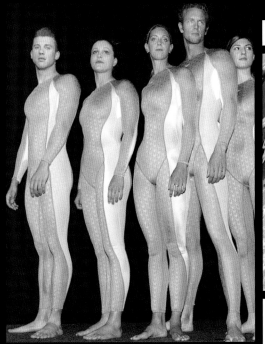

Five swimmers (*left*) model the Fastskin. An Olympic medalist (*above*) tries out the Fastskin in the water.

Full bodysuits delivered what their makers promised – a swimsuit that could shave vital seconds off a racer's time. The Fastskin full bodysuit was an immediate hit when it was introduced in the year 2000. Champion swimmers broke world records in these sharklike second skins.

Animals as Machines

The scientists who studied sharks to improve swimsuits were using the science of biomechanics. Biomechanics is all about learning from nature. Scientists study the bodies of living things as if those bodies were machines. Then they ask; 'How does this machine work?' They apply what they learn to technology, such as swimsuits and aeroplane wings.

The Wright Brothers also used biomechanics. They spent a lot of time observing birds in flight. They used their observations to help them design wings for the world's first successful motorized aircraft in 1903.

chapter 2

Have More Fun!

Some people see sports as a challenge. They train hard to be as good as they can be at competitive sports such as pole vaulting and bicycle racing. But most people use sports for recreation. They play recreational sports, such as throwing Frisbees and surfing, to get exercise and have a good time. Sports technology helps these people put more fun and adventure into their lives.

Flying Pie Tins

Not all sports equipment is built from space-age technology and months of careful scientific testing. Sometimes all it takes is a simple idea and a lucky accident. More than one hundred years ago, a bakery launched a fun new recreational sport without even knowing it.

It was their round pie tins that got things going. College students at Yale University loved the taste of the pies from the nearby Frisbie Pie Company in Bridgeport, USA. They also had fun spinning the empty Frisbie pie tins through the air and playing catch with them. 'Frisbie'! they would yell as a warning to anyone who got in the way.

The company was still producing Frisbie pies in 1948 when two inventors came up with an improved version of the Frisbie tin. Their plastic disc could fly much further with far more accuracy.

This is one of the original Frisbie Pie Company pie tins. 'Frisbie!'

The secret was the outer third of the disc, called the Morrison Slope in honour of one of the inventors. The way the Morrison Slope curled down and wrapped underneath made it act like an airplane wing, lifting the disc to soar through the air.

Here's how it works. As the disc flies along, the air moves faster up the slope on top. This creates low pressure above the disc. At the same time, the curled edge of the disc causes air to slow down beneath it. This results in higher pressure below the disc. These two pressure changes combine to keep the disc floating longer.

A modern Frisbee flies through the air further than the old pie tins because of the effect of the Morrison Slope.

Early versions were called Flying Saucers and Pluto Platters. Eventually they became known as Frisbees, in honour of the Frisbie Pie Company.

More than 200 million Frisbees have been sold. People throw them to their dogs as well as to one another. Frisbees also are used in their own unique sports. Ultimate Frisbee is a cross between football, rugby and basketball. Frisbee golf is played on professional courses from coast to coast.

Listen to the Riders

With the Frisbee, a new sport had been invented, but sports technology is just as important for keeping up with changing needs in existing sports.

This is especially true in skateboarding. The sport first took off decades ago when people nailed steel roller skate wheels to wooden planks. This combination made for a bumpy ride with little control. Later, clay wheels helped a little, but not much.

Finally, in the early 1970s, the first urethane wheels were invented. Urethane is a chemical compound that is soft enough to provide a smoother ride and strong enough to last a long time. Urethane wheels also grip the ground very well.

The invention of urethane wheels led to an explosion of the popularity of skateboarding in the 1970s. Boards then were shaped like snow skis. That's because riders were mostly zooming and zigzagging down hilly streets, like skiers on snowy hillsides.

IT'S A FACT!

The first urethane wheels were named Cadillacs, after the smooth-riding luxury American cars.

However, skateboarders' needs changed again when skateboard parks came along. In these parks, riders rode mostly in straight lines up and down steep inclines. This made straight-ahead speed more important than side-to-side movement. Responding to these changes, skateboards became blunt at the front and wider in the middle.

Then, in 1979, a lot of skateboarders left the parks and took to the streets, so boards got narrower. A skateboard designer named Tim Piumarta was one of the first to put curves into boards. He designed boards that turned upwards at front and back. They were also concave – curved upwards from side to side. These curves gave riders more control for riding and doing tricks on flat city pavements and kerbs.

In recent years, more skateboarders have been going back to the parks, which means more design changes.

Notice the shape of this skateboard. Skateboard designs change based on where the board will be ridden. This one is being used at a skateboard park.

Surfboards and Ecology

Not all sports technology is about performance. Technology can also help sports participants take care of the Earth.

Chris Hines of Cornwall, loves surfing. He also loves Earth's environment, and that makes him concerned about old, used surfboards that get thrown away and end up in landfills. He calls a modern surfboard a lump of horrible petrochemical plastic [that] will sit in landfill sites and have a negative environmental footprint'.

Modern surfboards contain oil-based chemicals that can poison the soil and water when they decompose. So Hines has designed a lightweight board wrapped in hemp cloth and coated with plant-based chemicals. He calls it the Eco Board because it's ecologically friendly. Old Eco Boards, with their natural materials, will decompose without harming the Earth.

Hanging in Air

What do you get when you combine high speed, great heights and motorless flight? You get the extreme sport of hang gliding. The ride begins on a high hill or cliff. If it's a hill, the pilot runs down the slope to get going. If it's a cliff, the pilot gets airborne by just jumping.

The airborne pilot hangs below the glider's V-shaped wing. As the glider picks up speed, air flows past the wing. The wing is designed so that air flows faster over the top of the wing than the bottom. Like a Frisbee with its Morrison Slope, the faster air lowers the air pressure above the wing. The slower air raises the pressure below it. The effect is a force called lift. Lift helps keep the glider aloft.

Hang gliders are shaped like a V, much like he V of a bird's wings.

Working against lift is gravity. Gravity pulls the glider down towards the ground, but also helps it move forwards. The more the glider moves forwards, the more air blows past and the more lift can be generated.

The last force that affects the glider is drag. Drag comes from the wing and its pilot colliding with air molecules. These trillions upon trillions of mid-air collisions create friction. That slows the glider down. Gravity and drag ensure that eventually the glider will land safely and the motorless ride will come to an end.

Meanwhile, the pilot turns the glider left and right by leaning this way or that. The pilot also controls the glider's altitude and speed. By pulling back, he tips the glider's nose downwards, causing the aircraft to speed up. By pushing forwards, he points the nose upwards, slowing the glider down.

Early hang gliders had heavy wooden frames. Then came lighter aluminium and carbon fibre frames. These were easier to manoevre.

Wing technology also changed. Instead of flexible fabric that flapped like a sail, many modern hang-glider wings are made of rigid metal that produces greater lift for longer flights.

How long? Flights of 7 hours covering 300 to 500 km (200 to 300 miles) have become common. In 2001 pilot Manfred Ruhmer flew his hang glider 695 km (432 miles) on a flight lasting 10.5 hours!

Flying Like an Eagle

The inventor of the first hang-gliding wing developed his invention during the 1960s for the US space programme. The V-shaped wing was supposed to guide space capsules back to Earth, but NASA decided to stick with parachutes.

Instead of going to waste, this aerial innovation took on a new life. A harness was added to the wing and the hang glider was born. People could enjoy the thrill of flying like eagles.

Skyflying

Not everyone wants to fall through space at 190 kph (120 mph), but for those who do, there's the extreme sport of skydiving. The diver jumps from inside a plane, wearing a parachute and helmet.

Veteran skydivers make their jumps at about 4,500 m above the Earth. That way, they get the added thrill of 60 seconds of free falling at about

190 kph (120 mph) before they must open their parachute and float gently to the ground. Free-falling skydivers face the ground with their belly pulled up in an arch, using their arms and legs to steer.

Skilled skydivers can try something even more daring during free fall. They can swoop and turn in different directions. It's called skyflying.

Some skyflyers wear specially designed flying suits for extra lift, control, and speed. Skyray, for example, is a triangle-shaped pair of carbon fibre wings that give skyflyers two minutes of free flying at speeds of about 300 to 500 kph (200 to 300 mph). That's as fast as the world's fastest bird, the peregrine falcon, can dive.

The skyflyer jumps from the plane headfirst to pick up speed. Then he or she grabs the handles on each wing, pulls them outwards, and shoots away. The added lift from the open wings gives the flyer the added speed and distance, until it's time to open the chute and return to the ground.

Some people refer to skyflyer's suits as birdman suits.

chapter 3

Be Safe and Comfortable

thletic apparel is a vital part of sports technology. What athletes wear can be crucial to success. Good apparel helps athletes stay safe and comfortable as they run, jump, ride and fall from the sky.

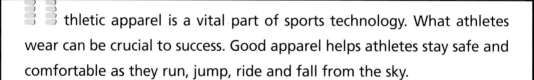

Soft Landings

Jumping from a plane thousands of metres above the ground is dangerous to say the least. But skydiving deaths are rare. Each year in the United Kingdom, about 40 people die in parachuting accidents. That's roughly one death for every 100,000 jumps.

It's hard to imagine a piece of sports technology more important to the wearer's safety than a parachute. After their 60 seconds of free fall, skydivers have descended to an altitude of about 1,200 m. They keep track of their height above Earth's surface with an instrument known as an altimeter, which is strapped to their arm.

Round parachutes are rarely used anymore. Instead, rectangular ram-air chutes provide skydivers better safety and control. Ram-air chutes are made of two layers of fabric, one on top of the other, connected by fabric ribs to make cells. These cells fill with air, so the chute looks something like an air mattress. They are made of ripstop nylon that is woven in a special way for safety. If the fabric should get a rip in it, crosshatched reinforcement threads will stop the rip from tearing any wider.

This is a ram-air parachute. It is easily manoeuvrable and makes landings

Ram-air chutes are easy to manoeuvre. Using left and right steering lines, one in each hand, even an amateur skydiver can land within a few metres of the target spot. Also the landing is so soft that when the target area is grassy or sandy, the skydiver can glide in barefoot. How's that for safety and comfort?

Skydivers wear helmets for the same reason American football players wear them – to protect their heads from injury. Even with helmets, modern players suffer more than 100,000 concussions a year. A concussion is a blow to the head that jars the brain inside the skull. Sometimes serious injuries can result.

People used to believe that the top of the head needed protecting the most. But researchers discovered that the most harmful hits were actually delivered to the side of the head or face. Therefore helmet technology changed. Riddell, sports equipment manufacturer constructed the Revolution helmet. Specially designed pads line the sides of the helmet to absorb the energy from sideways blows. The curve of the helmet shell was designed by computer to more efficiently absorb hits.

Helmets, like this one, help protect players in the National Football League, in the USA, but they don't stop all injuries.

Tests showed that this new helmet cut down on the number of concussions. But researchers warned that the helmet did not eliminate injuries. 'There is no such thing as a concussion-proof helmet,' one expert said.

Tough Guys

American football players haven't always worn helmets. A hundred years ago, football was a wild, brutal sport with lots of fights that led to lots of injuries.

Some players grew their hair long to help cushion blows to the head. Most players didn't dare wear a helmet. Gerald Ford, 38th president of the United States, played college football at the University of Michigan from 1932 to 1934, and he never wore a helmet. Those who did risked being called wimps.

Finally, by the 1940s players had to wear helmets. That was the rule. The first helmets were leather. Then came plastic helmets lined with foam. During the 1970s, air cushions were added inside the crown of the helmet with valves on top for pumping in air. Before taking the field, players had queue up to get their helmets filled. This pumped-up head-gear helped soften the impact of a collision.

This American football player from the 1940s wears a leather helmet.

Computers Detecting Head Injuries

The worst thing an American football player can do after getting a head injury is to get another one soon after it. This can happen if an injured player stays in the game after getting hurt. Another head injury can lead to serious problems. If the player didn't suffer brain damage the first time, the chances of damage from later hits goes way up. This is especially true for young athletes.

This scientist has been keeping track of head injuries using electronic encoder modules in American footballers' helmets.

At a secondary school in the USA scientists are working to prevent serious head injuries to American football players. The scientists equipped players' helmets with electronic encoder modules. As soon as a player takes a hit to the head, the modules wirelessly beam information about the hit to a laptop computer on the sidelines.

The information includes the location of the hit and how hard the blow was. If the player takes a serious hit, he won't be allowed back in the game. When athletes are diagnosed with a concussion, researchers look at what type of hit caused it. These scientists hope to learn a lot more about brain injuries and how to prevent them.

Shoes and Waffles

A revolution in running-shoe technology began one morning in 1971 in the kitchen of a house outside of Eugene, Oregon, USA. Bill Bowerman sat watching his wife Barbara cooking waffles.

Bowerman was hungry, but when his wife slid the waffles onto his plate, he just stared. He couldn't stop staring. His attention was locked on the waffles' texture, the little squares that covered each one. What was he thinking as he stared at those waffles?

He was thinking about the bottom sole of a shoe. He was thinking about speed, grip, tread and traction.

Everyday things such as waffles can lead to big innovations such as the textured outsole on this running shoe.

Bowerman soon put his thoughts into action. He poured liquid rubber into a waffle-making mould to create the first crude prototype for the bottom of the modern running shoe. Bowerman marketed the shoes and, in a short time, became co-founder and president of Nike.

Look at the bottom sole of a running shoe. It's called the outsole. Fifty years ago, it would have been smooth – and slippery. Today, the outsole's waffle-like texture grips the ground, giving the runner a sure, firm stride – no slipping.

Shoes and Shock

For runners, softening the impact with the running surface is vital. In a way, shoes are like helmets. They must soften impact to protect the runner's feet and legs from getting sore and injured. How could sports shoes do a better job of giving that protection? Manufacturers began asking this question during the 1970s.

To find answers, they hired experts to research how humans run. The researchers learned how shock waves affect feet and ankles each time the runner's foot hits the ground. The manufacturers used this information to help them find ways to cushion that shock.

One answer was a plastic material named EVA (short for ethylene vinyl acetate). The EVA plastic was full of tiny air bubbles. When it was put inside the heels of shoes, it helped cushion the shock of running.

The air pump was another innovation. A shock-cushioning air bag was set into the sole of the shoe. Later on, a pump valve was added so that wearers could pump up their shoes like bicycle tyres.

That was back in the 1980s. Modern running shoes have all sorts of cushioning systems, including air capsules, gel capsules, foam and moulded plastic.

Socks and Sweat

Even socks have been engineered to help the runner. The key factor is taking care of sweaty feet. As feet sweat, perspiration makes them slippery and uncomfortable. As the sweat soaks into the socks, they become wet and heavy, slowing the runner down.

Sports sock makers looked for ways to keep runners' feet and socks comfortably free of perspiration. They hired researchers to investigate the science of sweating in order to develop socks with superior wicking powers. Wicking is the act of absorbing sweat and moving it away from the skin. Modern sports socks are designed to wick. A layer of fabric on the inside of the sock attracts sweat, pulling it away from the runner's foot. The sweat is then wicked, or passed on, to a layer on the outside of the sock. From there, it can simply evaporate into the air, leaving the runner's feet and socks perspiration free.

IT'S A FACT!

Some T-shirts also are designed with wicking technology. These keep you from soaking your shirt when running or participating in other sports. Some experts worry that wicking T-shirts can be unhealthy, though. If sweat is wicked off the skin, it can't do its job, which is to cool the body. The body then produces more sweat to cool itself. Eventually, some say, dehydration and overheating can occur.

These professional ice hockey players are showing off their new uniforms that wick away moisture.

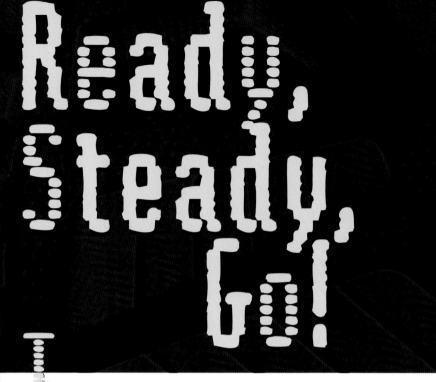

Ready, Steady, Go!

Think of all the competitive athletes whose success depends on time. Sprinters, marathon runners, cyclists, racing car drivers, downhill skiers, speed skaters, swimmers and rowers – the winner is the one who completes the course in the least amount of time.

As athletes get faster and faster, accurate timing becomes more crucial. In competitive sports such as sprinting and swimming, for instance, the difference between winning and losing can be tiny. It may be measured in tenths, hundredths and even thousandths of a second. How can these tiny moments of time be captured?

Capturing Time

In races that take place on land, a tiny glass capsule known as a transponder measures the time an athlete takes to complete a race. The transponder is worn in a chin strap or around the ankle like an ankle bracelet.

Inside the transponder is a timing chip that is similar to the chips used in computers. Inside the chip is an energizing coil. When it's activated, the coil causes the chip to transmit an electrical signal. This happens when an athlete reaches special mats laid out at the finish line. Antennae in the mat pick up the signal and send it to computers, which collect and store it.

The signal contains two vital pieces of information. It identifies the person wearing the chip and it tells the exact moment in time that the wearer crossed the finish line.

Photo Finish

Just to be sure, some races use a backup timing system as well. Video cameras take pictures of the finish line at the moment that each contestant crosses it.

This backup system is called slit video. That's because the cameras capture just a slit of the finish line: an up-and-down, super-thin slice, 0.2 millimetres wide. That's about as thick as eight human hairs. Each camera takes as many as 2,000 of these super-thin images per second. That's one picture every 0.0005 second.

Let's say the race is a sprint, with most of the runners crossing the finish line within a split second of one another. The slit video cameras will show the runners, from head to toe, crossing the line a tiny bit at a time. First, the tip of the toe . . . then the tip of the nose . . . then a fingertip . . . an eyelash . . . and so forth. The camera lenses are so sharp that they can pick up each individual hair on a runner's body.

These thousands of slit images are stored in computers. In a matter of seconds, computer software assembles them all together. The end result is a photo finish – a complete picture of the runners crossing the finish line in the order they reached it.

Sensors and Touch Pads

When competitive swimmers get set for a race, they climb up onto starting blocks. Inside the blocks are electronic sensors. Sensors come in different types. Some types respond to heat or light. The sensors used in swimming races respond to pressure. The moment the swimmer's feet leave the block, the sensor records that moment in time.

As the swimmers speed through the water in their separate lanes, plastic touch pads await each of them. These super thin pads are attached to the wall at either end of the pool, just below the surface.

A touch pad is something like a doorbell. The moment the swimmer's fingertip touches it, a sensor like the ones in the starting blocks responds, recording that moment in time.

Like running races, swimming races can be extremely close. Swimmers sometimes finish within hundredths of a second of one another. For backup, high-speed cameras record the start and finish of each race.

Infrared Light

As far as timing goes, the start of a race is as crucial as the finish. No one may leave the starting line before that one moment in time when the race officially begins.

In speed skating competition, an electronic starting pistol is used. As the pistol in the starter's hand gives off a loud crack, the pistol's tip shows a

This starting pistol was used to start a men's speed skating final at the 2006 Winter Olympics.

flash of bright light. Skaters may choose to concentrate on the sound, the light or both to make sure they take off at exactly the right moment.

A special speed skating timer records the finish time for each competitor. Known as a photo beam unit, this timer depends on infrared light. Infrared light is made of light waves invisible to the human eye. The unit projects a continuous beam of infrared light across the finish line. The moment a skater breaks this beam, a signal is sent to the timer and the skater's exact finish time is recorded.

Twenty-five Stopwatches

What was timing technology like before chips, sensors, infrared photo beams and computers recorded exact times? The best technology available before computers was a stopwatch. This watch can be instantly started and stopped by pushing a button. Stopwatches were used to time competitive running events.

A total of 25 stopwatches were used, held by 25 people standing at the finish line. Just as the first runner crossed the line, all 25 clicked their stopwatches to capture the moment.

However, they would never all click them at exactly the same moment. People are unique. They all have different reaction times. Inevitably, some clicks would come a few tenths of a second before or after others. So the 25 results were all written down and averaged. That average became the official winning time.

Training Athletes

Good training makes for good athletes. Before computers, athletic training focused on physical activity: running, lifting weights and working out, but computers gave training a new dimension.

Sensors and Laptops

If you ever see a swimmer with wires running from her suit to a laptop computer by the pool, you'll know that she's in training. A special computer training system is measuring her mechanics, the movements she makes during the act of swimming.

Swimming uses lots of different movements, from head to toe. Swimmers can't always tell what they're doing well and what they're not doing so well. With this computerized system, every stroke and every kick can be analyzed. That's because electronic sensors strapped to the swimmer's suit and connected to the wires record her movements. How far does she reach with each stroke? How much time does she take between strokes?

The answers to questions like these tell competitive swimmers what they are doing right and what they could do better. Even just taking a tiny bit too long gliding between strokes can add up. One swimmer said, 'I didn't realize how much slower it was making me. It shows you the little things that can make a difference.' One coach calls the system a cutting-edge tool.

Pitchers and Cameras

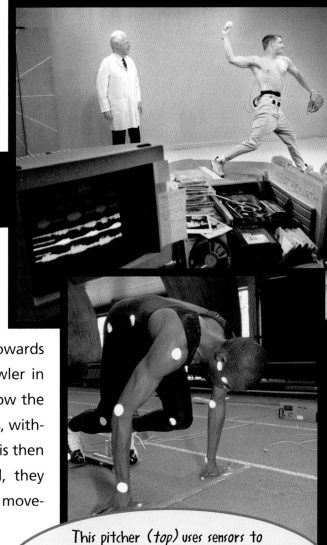

Baseball pitchers have something in common with swimmers – mechanics. The pitcher is the player on the fielding team who throws the ball towards the batter – a bit like the bowler in cricket. The pitcher trys to throw the ball past the batter three times, without him hitting it. If they do this then the batter is out. To do well, they must perform a sequence of movements in the right way.

Researchers in Texas, USA, use computers and cameras

This pitcher (top) uses sensors to improve his mechanics. A track athlete (bottom) uses reflective discs and a videocamera, known as motion capture, to improve his performance at the starting block.

to help pitchers improve their mechanics. As they throw, tiny reflective discs on their uniforms highlight their mechanics for the cameras. Twelve cameras record each pitch at 150 images per second. The images are put into a computer which converts them into a 3-D model. Then the pitcher's mechanics can be viewed from any angle to show what he's doing wrong.

When a pitcher is having problems, he looks at images of himself taken at a time when his pitching mechanics were perfect. By comparing those images with images from the present, he can see what he is doing differently. Then he can work on correcting his mechanics.

Sports technology also helps batsmen in cricket. Bowling machines give batsman the chance to practise batting against all the different types of delivery that could be bowled by an opposition bowler, and this bowler never gets tired!

Of course none of these machines actually look or behave quite like a human bowler, but they can come very close. The 2008 BOLA Professional

The ProBatter Professional Pitching Machine (above) is similar to the Abner Batter Training System. The ball comes out through a screen so players can see the release.

Bowling machine can replicate nearly every single bowling technique employed by a human bowler, from the subtle spin bowl to the 150 kph (90 mph) yorker.

Brilliant Boots

Football is a sport where the players depend upon skill, technique, strength, fitness and rigorous training to win matches. There is, however, another element involved — their kit.

The most important pieces of kit that footballers wears are, of course, their boots. Football boots have evolved a great deal over the last hundred years and hundreds of different types are available on the market.

Perhaps the most famous and one of the most popular types of modern football boot is the Adidas Predator. This boot was designed by the former Liverpool player, an Australian, Craig Johnston. Originally the predator boots had a number of teeth-like lumps on the top of the boot, the area where the ball is kicked. This design allowed for greater ball control, and the shape of the boot as well as its light weight design provided more swerve and power.

The latest model of Adidas's hi-tech Predator football boot.

chapter 6

Engineering Athletes

ony Volpentest was born without feet, but that didn't stop him from becoming a champion sprinter. Volpentest is one of a growing number of engineered athletes who have performed beyond their natural ability with the assistance of modern technology.

Space-Age Limbs

Artificial feet extend Volpentest's legs. Both the feet and the sockets that connect them to the legs are made of a

Tony Volpentest wins the Paralympic gold medal in the men's 200-metre race in 1996.

carbon-graphite composite. Thanks to the movable socket and a special flexed toe, the feet act like springboards. Each time Volpentest's foot hits the track, it springs back up and pushes him ahead, like a runner on two human feet.

Volpentest is one of thousands who compete in the Paralympics. These are Olympic-style games for athletes with a disability. Volpentest has won Paralympics gold medals in both the 100-metre and 200-metre runs. His times of 11.63 and 23.07 seconds are only a few seconds slower than the times of Olympic winners.

Oscar Pistorius also runs on artificial limbs. He has run the 100 metre in an even faster time than Volpentest. Pistorius runs on Cheetahs, a pair of J-shaped carbon fibre blades that give his legs extra spring and lengthen his stride. He calls himself 'the fastest man on no legs'.

Oscar Pistorius (above) sprints faster than most people with two feet, but he does so on Cheetahs (right).

Unfair Advantage?

Pistorius would like to compete in the Olympic Games against sprinters with human feet and legs. However, some people think he should not be allowed to run in races with Olympic athletes. They argue that Olympic rules forbid technological aids such as springs and wheels, since they would give the athlete an artificial advantage. Olympic sports are all about natural human ability, not technological engineering.

Pistorius's supporters agree that the Cheetahs do give Pistorius extra spring. However, they point out, carbon-fibre limbs are still less efficient than natural legs. As a result, Cheetahs would not really give Pistorius an unfair advantage over other Olympic runners.

His supporters have another argument: Hasn't sports technology already changed what we mean by 'natural'? Don't nearly all pole vaulters, runners, swimmers and other competitive athletes use high-tech equipment and clothing that make them better? Nobody complains about that. So why should Pistorius and other athletes with artificial limbs be kept from competing in the Olympics?

Genetic Engineering

Experts predict that another kind of engineered athlete is about to appear on the sports scene. These athletes will be engineered by scientists from the inside out.

The key is genes, the trillions of microscopic chemical units within your cells that tell your body how to grow and behave. If your genes were changed, you would grow and behave differently. The process of changing genes is called genetic engineering.

Competitive athletes are always trying to get better. What if normal genes could be replaced by superior genes to make tall athletes even taller? Strong ones even stronger? Fast ones even faster?

Into the Future

Genetic engineering is still in the experimental stage. Researchers work with laboratory animals rather than humans.

This mouse was genetically engineered by this scientist. One day this technology could be used on humans.

IT'S A FACT!

The World Anti-Doping Agency (WADA) determines which substances, such as steroids, are banned in international sports competitions. Although they don't believe athletes are experimenting with gene altering yet, WADA officials have already declared gene altering illegal.

Some experts predict that one day soon, genetic engineering will be safe and easy to perform, and then athletes will take advantage of it. One expert even believes that one day, 'Somebody who's not athletic at all could be transformed into something superhuman.'

Our journey through the world of sports technology must end here, looking out into the future. Will we be watching genetically engineered super-athletes compete someday? How much swifter and stronger will athletes become? How much higher will they be able to jump and fly? At this time, it looks like the sky's the limit.

Glossary

aerodynamics: the study of how air flows around a moving body

biomechanics: the scientific study of how the bones and muscles of humans and animals move

carbon fibre: thread-like strands of carbon atoms sealed in heated plastic

composite: two or more materials that are bound together to make a new material

concussion: a blow to the head that jars the brain inside the skull

drag: the resistance an object meets while travelling through air or water

free fall: the time between the moment when a skydiver leaves an aeroplane to the moment the skydiver activates a parachute

friction: resistance that happens when one body comes in contact with another

gene: microscopic chemical units within cells that tell a person's body how to grow and behave

genetic engineering: the process of changing genes so that the body will behave differently in some specific way

hang gliding: a sport in which a pilot in a harness hanging from the wing of a glider controls the glider's flight by shifting body weight

infrared light: a wave of light that is invisible to the human eye

Kevlar: space-age material that is five times stronger than steel; it is used in tennis rackets, golf clubs and other sports equipment

lift: force that acts on the flow of air over a wing that creates an upwards thrust opposite to the downwards pull of gravity

manuoevrable: capable of easily changing position

mechanics: scientific study of the effect of forces and energy on bodies; the movements that athletes make as they play their sport

Paralympics: Olympic-style games for athletes with disabilities

petrochemicals: chemicals made from oil, natural gas, coal or other fossil fuels

prototype: an original model for a new invention

sensor: a device that responds to a change by producing an electrical signal

skydiving: a sport in which a person jumps from a plane, falls freely and then breaks the fall with a parachute

sports technology: tools, machines and materials used by people who play sports

technique: a certain method used to perform a specific task

titanium: a strong, lightweight space-age metal that is silvery grey in colour

touch pad: a thin pad just below the water at each end of a lane in a pool used to record a swimmer's time electronically

wicking: the act of moving sweat away from skin and fabric

Source Notes

p. 18, Skewed View, 'Chris Hines Interview,' *CNN.com*, 29 August 2007, http://edition.cnn.com/2007/BUSINESS/08/30/hines.interview/index.html (3 January 2008).

p. 24, WebMD, 'New Helmet Technology May Reduce Football Head Injuries,' *FoxNews.com*, January 10, 2006, http://www.foxnews.com/story/0,2933,181209,00.html (January 2008).

p. 35, Alicia Caldwell, 'Technology Helping Swimmers Improve,' *St. Petersburg Times*, 27 August 2000, http://www.sptimes.com/News/082700/Sports/Technology_helping_sw.shtml (3 January 2008).

Selected Bibliography

Abrams, Michael. 'Wingman.' *Wired Magazine*. September 2003. http://www.wired. com/wired/archive/11.09/wing.html (3 January 2008).

Aspen Historical Society. "From Tip to Tale." *Aspen Historical Society*. N.d. http:// www.aspenhistory.org/tipchp2b.html (3 January 2008).

Bellis, Mary. "The First Flight of the Frisbee." *About.com: Inventors*. 2007. http:// inventors.about.com/library/weekly/aa980218.htm (3 January 2008).

Jenkins, M. *Materials in Sports Equipment*. London: CRC, 2003.

Lamb, Gregory M. 'Will Gene-Altered Athletes Kill Sport?' *Christian Science Monitor*. 23 August 2004. http://www.csmonitor.com/2004/0823/p12s01-stgn.html (3 January 2008).

McNichol, Tom. 'The Ultimate Pitching Machine.' *Wired Magazine*. June 2004. http:// www.wired.com/wired/archive/12.06/strikeout_pr.html (3 January 2008).

The Olympic Games: Athens 1896–Athens 2004. New York: DK Adult, 2004.

Russel, Gordon W. *Sports Science Secrets: From Myth to Facts*. Victoria, BC: Trafford Publishing, 2006.

Science Daily. 'High School Football Players Wear Special Helmets to Monitor Brain Injuries.' 3 October 2007. http://www.sciencedaily.com/releases/2007/09/070927121109.htm (3 January 2008).

– – –. 'Newer Football Helmet Design May Reduce Incidence of Concussions in High School Players, Shows University of Pittsburgh Study.' 14 January 2006. http:// www.sciencedaily.com/releases/2006/01/060114151826.htm (3 January 2008).

Sinha, Alex. 'Chip Timing – What It Does and How It Works.' *Marathonguide.com*. n.d. http://www.marathonguide.com/features/Articles/RaceTimingWithChip.cfm (3 January 2008).

Tamburrini, C. *Genetic Technology and Sport*. London: Routledge, 2005.

Tomlinson, Joe. *Extreme Sports*. London: Carlton Books, 2002.

Further Reading and Websites

De Winter, James. Extreme Science: Secrets of Sport: The Technology That Makes Champions (Extreme!) 2008.

Donaldson, Chris. Skydive: Sport Parachuting Explained The Crowood Press Ltd, 2000.

Guile Melanie. Olympic Games 2008 - History of the Olympic Games Heinemann Library, 2008.

Hammond, Tim. Sports (DK Eyewitness Books) Dorling Kindersley Publishers Ltd., 2005.

Hornby, Hugh and Sarah Phillips. Football (Eyewitness) Dorling Kindersley Publishers Ltd., 2004

Horsley, Andy. Skateboarding Hodder Wayland, 2001.

Jango-Cohen. Judith. Bionics (Cool Science) Lerner Publishing Group, Inc., 2008.

Mackay, Francis and Dave Burroughs. The History of Football (Football Kit) Hopscotch Educational Publishing, 2001.

McCann, Liam. The Olympics: Facts, Figures and Fun (Facts Figures & Fun) Photographers' Press Ltd, 2006.

Michael, Dean. Extreme Sports Penguin, 2008.

Radnedge, Keir. ITV Sport Complete Encyclopedia of Football Carlton Books Ltd, 2007.

Rita, Storey. Cycling (Know Your Sport) Franklin Watts, 2008.

Royston, Angela. Plastic: Let's Look at the Frisbee Heinemann Library, 2005.

Whittal, Noel. Hand Gliding and Paragliding (Xtreme Sports) Ticktock Media Ltd., 2008.

Skateboard Science

http://www.exploratorium.edu/skateboarding/skatedesign.html

Learn all about how skateboards were developed, how they work, and what they're made of. A video interview with a skateboard designer is included.

Speedo International: Fastskin

http://www.speedointernational.com

This is the official website for the fastskin body suit. With information about all of the technology and innovations in the fastskin as well as numerous other specialist swimwear products.

British Hang Gliding and Paragliding Association

http://www.bhpa.co.uk/

This site for the British Hang Gliding and Paragliding association is a guide to everything involved in hang gliding and paragliding. It explains the science behind the sport as well offering information on where the best places in Britain are to do it, where you can have lessons, what equipment you'll need and how much it will cost.

Index

About the Author

Ron Fridell has written for radio, television, and newspapers. He has also written books about the Human Genome Project, including *Decoding Life: Unraveling the Mysteries of the Genome*; and on genetics, including *Genetic Engineering* in the Cool Science series; as well as on using DNA to solve crimes. In addition to writing books, Fridell regularly visits libraries and schools to conduct workshops on non-fiction writing.